CITIES OF THE WORLD

DUBLIN

BY DEBORAH KENT

CHILDREN'S PRESS®
A Division of Grolier Publishing
New York London Hong Kong Sydney
Danbury, Connecticut

CONSULTANTS

Albert Ronan
Vice President, Shamrock American Club
Past Vice President, Dublin American Association
Member, Irish American Heritage Society

Linda Cornwell
Learning Resource Consultant
Indiana Department of Education

Project Director: Downing Publishing Services
Design Director: Karen Kohn & Associates, Ltd.
Photo Researcher: Jan Izzo
Pronunciations: Courtesy of Tony Breed, M.A., Linguistics, University of Chicago

> NOTES ON IRISH PRONUNCIATION
> Irish, or Gaelic, is a difficult language to pronounce correctly. The pronunciations
> in this book are simplified because there are many sounds in Irish that do not occur
> in English. The words are pronounced basically the way the pronunciation guides
> look. There are a few notes, however: *ah* is like *a* in father; *a* is as in can; *ay* is as in
> day; *ow* is always as in cow, never as in tow; *ghee* is like the *gea* in gear; <u>h</u> is a sound
> that does not occur in English. It is like the *h* in hat but stronger and harsher. If you
> try to say *k* as in kite but relax and slur the sound, it will sound like <u>h</u>.

Library of Congress Cataloging-in-Publication Data

Kent, Deborah
    Dublin / by Deborah Kent.
        p. cm. — (Cities of the world)
    Includes index.
    Summary: Describes physical aspects, history, and social life and customs
of the capital of the Republic of Ireland.
    ISBN 0-516-20302-9 (lib.bdg.)   0-516-26144-4 (pbk.)
    1. Dublin (Ireland)—Juvenile literature. [1. Dublin (Ireland)]
  I. Title.   II. Series: Cities of the world (New York, N.Y.)
DA995.D75K28   1997   96-35454
941.8'35—dc20   CIP
                                                    AC

TABLE OF CONTENTS

There is a spot on O'Connell Street that is a Dublin meeting place. Each afternoon, young people join their friends at the Anna Livia Fountain to plan their evening's fun. Their voices mingle with the splash of water, the chatter of birds, and the steady rumble of traffic.

Left: A night view of O'Connell Street and the bridge over the River Liffey

Below: A Dublin resident

O'Connell Street sprawls 150 feet wide and flows with six lanes of traffic. It is one of the broadest city streets in Europe. Down the center stretches an island of grass and trees, a welcome strip of green in a sea of pavement. The trees are a safe haven for huge flocks of black-and-white birds called wagtails. The chattering wagtails are among Dublin's many symbols.

Here and there along the island, a granite spire soars skyward. Green with age, bronze statues tower on pedestals. These statues and monuments honor the heroes of Dublin's proud, sorrowful past.

Dublin is the capital of the Republic of Ireland, or Eire, which has been an independent nation since 1922. The city lies on the Irish Sea at the mouth of the River Liffey. During the twentieth century, Dublin underwent vast expansion. In the heart of the city, old neighborhoods vanished to make way for blocks of offices and apartments. The city spread farther and farther into the surrounding countryside. Fields and pastures disappeared beneath highways and waves of suburban homes.

Despite these changes, Dubliners cherish their history. For nearly 1,000 years, Ireland was occupied by foreign powers. The people of Dublin kept their traditions alive through songs, dance, and legends. Time and again, they rose in armed rebellion against their oppressors. Each uprising produced new heroes, men and women who fought and often died for the cause of Irish freedom.

Many of these Dublin heroes are remembered in stone and bronze on O'Connell Street. There is a monument to Charles Parnell, a nineteenth-century leader who is sometimes called the Uncrowned King of Ireland. Another statue celebrates labor leader Jim Larkin. Its inscription bears Larkin's stirring words, "The great appear great because we are on our knees. Let us rise."

Above: The view from Howth Head Lighthouse, in a suburb just north of Dublin, is one of the most beautiful in the world.

Left: The Anna Livia Fountain

I n 1914, writer James Joyce published a collection of short stories entitled *Dubliners*. Joyce had a great gift for storytelling. He found tragedy and beauty in the lives of ordinary Dublin men and women. Joyce wrote about the deep religious faith of his characters, their struggles with poverty, and their delightful humor.

Dublin (or *Dooblin*, as Dubliners pronounce it) has changed a great deal since Joyce's time. But the character of its people remains very much the same.

THE PEOPLE OF DUBLIN

People have lived on the site of today's Dublin for at least 4,000 years. The earliest inhabitants belonged to a little-known tribe called the Firbolg. The Firbolg were eventually driven away by Celtic people from present-day France and Spain. The Celts spoke a language called Gaelic. In the twelfth century A.D., invaders from England crossed the Irish Sea and conquered Ireland. English settlers continued to pour in during the centuries that followed. Though they often intermarried with the Celtic Irish, these "Anglo-Irish" people kept a separate identity. Most Dubliners today have both Celtic and English ancestors. English has almost completely replaced the Gaelic language. Yet Dubliners feel themselves to be the keepers of a proud Irish heritage.

Until the early twentieth century, Ireland was a land of small farms. But more and more people left the land and moved to the cities. Today, about one-fourth of the people in the Republic of Ireland live in Dublin and its suburbs. Dublin has about 750,000 people, making it roughly the same size as the American city of San Francisco. Dubliners are often referred to as "Dubs," or "Jackeens."

Though this family still runs a farm, many Irish farm families have left the land and moved to cities like Dublin.

Gaelic (GAY-lick)
Shelta (SHELL-tuh)

*Irish children at a
Dublin street fair*

The Traveling People

In bygone times, families of Tinkers wandered over Ireland in horse-drawn wagons. They lived by mending pots, pans, and kettles. Like the Gypsies, Ireland's Tinkers form a distinct ethnic group with unique customs. A few still speak an ancient language called Shelta. Today, many Tinkers live a fairly settled life in Dublin. They work at odd jobs or sell secondhand goods on the street. Painted wagons have disappeared, replaced by trailers and pickup trucks.

Flowing from west to east, the River Liffey cuts Dublin into two sections. The region north of the Liffey is usually called North Dublin. South Dublin is everything south of the river. Much of North Dublin is laid out in a grid-like pattern with straight, wide streets. North Dublin has some areas of terrible poverty. Jobs are in short supply. Crime is a growing menace. Yet parks and playgrounds brighten the poorest neighborhoods. North Dublin has some of the liveliest, most colorful areas of the city.

The River Liffey, shown here at the O'Connell Street Bridge, is the dividing line between North Dublin and South Dublin.

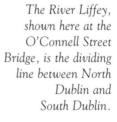

During the late eighteenth century, Dublin expanded southward. South Dublin arose as the domain of wealthy Anglo-Irish families. It has pleasant, tree-lined streets and many elegant homes. North Dubliners, however, sometimes claim it lacks character and flair.

Every city has its eccentrics—men and women who disregard society's rules. Over the years, Dublin has had more than its share of them. There was Robert Maire Symllie, editor of the *Irish Times*. Wearing a green sombrero, Symllie walked the streets, singing lead articles in an operatic baritone. Another man, who called himself Endymion, always dressed in white. He carried a compass, an alarm clock, and a pair of sabers. Lifting his sabers on high, he saluted statues and passersby.

Most Dubliners are very tolerant toward such unusual behavior. It simply adds a bit of color to the fabric of Dublin life.

Schoolchildren on an outing in the park at Merrion Square

An eccentric man who called himself Endymion used to dress all in white and walk the streets of Dublin carrying a compass and a pair of sabers.

WHERE THE TIME GOES

"The man who invented time made plenty of it," runs a saying in Dublin. Dublin streets are clogged with traffic. Everyone seems to be hurrying somewhere. Yet compared with other big cities, Dublin has a leisurely pace. People still find time to read the newspaper in the park or to have a cup of tea with their neighbors. And, naturally, they have time to relax at the corner pub.

A pub, or public house, is a tavern. But a Dublin pub is far more than a place where beer and whiskey are served. In the corner pub, neighbors meet to discuss current events, argue about politics, and exchange local gossip. Light meals, called "pub grub," consist of thick bread with ham or cheese. By law, children are forbidden to enter a pub, but the rule is seldom enforced. In most pubs, the whole family is welcome.

As evening at the pub wears on, someone suddenly breaks into song. Talk slides to a halt, and more voices blend with the first. Soon, nearly everyone is singing. The songs are familiar to all. There are "The Bold Fenian Men," "Irish Rover," and of course that old favorite which begins,

A Dublin couple reading the newspaper together in St. Stephen's Green

In Dublin's fair city,
Where the girls are so pretty,
I first set my eyes on sweet Molly Malone.
She wheeled her wheelbarrow
Through streets broad and narrow,
Crying, "Cockles and mussels!
Alive, alive O!"

This Irish girl may resemble the legendary
Molly Malone, who once sold shellfish called
mussels (above) in the streets of Dublin.

KEEPING THE FAITH

Every evening at six, Dublin's state radio station broadcasts a peal of three church bells. This is the Angelus, a traditional call to prayer in the Roman Catholic Church. The Angelus bells remind Dubliners to pause for a moment of religious contemplation. Whether they are rushing home from work, cooking supper, or practicing on the soccer field, Dubliners remember that life has a spiritual side.

Most Dubliners are Roman Catholics. Catholicism touches nearly every aspect of life in the city. Dublin is dotted with churches great and small. Many children attend Catholic schools. When Dubliners plan to meet tomorrow at noon, they usually add the words, "Please God." If the name of a deceased friend comes up in conversation, a Dubliner crosses herself and murmurs, "God rest his soul." To emphasize a point, she exclaims, "By Heaven and all the saints!"

Among the pillars of the Catholic Church, none is more revered in Dublin than Saint Patrick. According to legend, Patrick was born in Scotland. He was captured by pirates when he was a boy, sometime during the fifth century A.D. The pirates took him to Ireland. At that time, the people of Ireland followed an ancient religion with many gods and goddesses. Patrick lived as a slave in Ireland until he escaped to France. In A.D. 432, he returned to spread the Christian religion. According to

Celtic cross

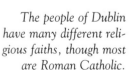

The people of Dublin have many different religious faiths, though most are Roman Catholic.

According to legend, St. Patrick preached on the spot where St. Patrick's Cathedral now stands.

legend, he preached on the spot where Dublin's St. Patrick's Cathedral now stands. According to another story, Saint Patrick proved God's power by driving all of the snakes out of Ireland. Ireland is the only country in the world with no native snake species.

Matt Talbot (1856-1925) is another important religious figure in Dublin. As a young man, Talbot worked on North Dublin's docks. Like most of the men on the waterfront, he was a drinker and a brawler. One day, Talbot saw a dog licking at a broken whiskey bottle. He realized he was living no better than that half-starved dog. He stopped drinking and spent the rest of his life in prayer. Poverty and alcoholism are problems for many Dubliners, as they were for Matt Talbot. Talbot's story affects Dubliners so deeply that many regard him as a saint.

Protestants are a religious minority in Dublin. Most are of British descent. The British occupied Ireland for more than 700 years. The story of this occupation, and of Irish efforts to resist it, is the story of Dublin itself.

Dubliners, like most of the Irish throughout the country, feel a deep connection with their past. They lament the sorrows of their ancestors, and praise their brave heroes. In Dublin, history is not a heap of dusty relics. It is a living presence, never to be forgotten.

THE GOLDEN AGE

"The wind is rough tonight, tossing the white hair of the ocean. I do not fear the fierce Vikings coursing the Irish Sea." Sometime during the eighth century A.D., an Irish monk scribbled these words on the edge of a page he was illustrating. At that time, the spiritual life of Ireland revolved around its monasteries. Monks traveled the land, spreading the word of God. Some crossed the sea to serve as missionaries throughout Europe.

The monasteries were also thriving centers of learning. The monks were among the few people in Ireland who knew how to read and write. Books were few, and each one was very precious. The printing press had not yet been invented. The only way to make a second copy of a book was to copy out each page by hand. Some monks devoted their lives to this painstaking work. Not only did they copy manuscripts that might be hundreds of pages long. They also filled them with splendid pictures, rich with vivid detail. Very slowly, book by book, the monks created priceless libraries.

Before the invention of the printing press, monks and other scholars copied manuscripts by hand.

A Dublin Treasure

Every day, visitors to Dublin's Trinity College stand in awe before the Book of Kells. Created by monks during the eighth and ninth centuries, the Book of Kells is a lavishly illustrated version of the Gospels of the New Testament. Every page is enhanced with beautiful pictures. The detail is so minute that it can best be seen with the help of a microscope.

Today, Dubliners look back on this era of learned monks as the Golden Age. During the Golden Age, the place where Saint Patrick preached was considered holy ground. Sometime in the fifth century A.D., a church arose on this site in Saint Patrick's honor.

Artist Michael Carroll uses gold leaf and pens such as these to create original Celtic art (left) based on the Book of Kells. He hand letters and paints in much the same way as Irish monks of 1,000 years ago.

In A.D. 837, a band of Viking warriors, or Norsemen, sailed to Ireland from present-day Norway. The Vikings landed at the mouth of the Liffey, where they established a fortified settlement. From this base, they sent raiding parties all over Ireland. Although people had lived in this area for centuries, the Viking settlement is considered the true origin of today's Dublin. The settlement took its name from two Gaelic words, *dubh* and *linn*, meaning "Black Pool." The name apparently refers to a pool in the Liffey.

Warriors from Norway, who sailed to Ireland in Viking ships like these, established a settlement on the site of what is now Dublin.

The Vikings destroyed many of Ireland's monasteries. They burned most of the precious books. The people of Ireland lived in constant terror. In 1014, the high king of Ireland, Brian Boru, organized an uprising against the invaders. In a fierce battle at Clontarf (now a Dublin suburb), he led the Irish to a ringing victory. For a while, the Vikings were driven back. But the Irish soon faced yet another invasion. This time, the enemy came from the island that lay to the east across the Irish Sea.

Brian Boru, the high king of Ireland, was killed in the Battle of Clontarf.

dubh (DUHV)
linn (LING)
Brian Boru (BREEN BUH-ROO)
Clontarf (KLUNN-TARF)

REBELS AND REPRISALS

The Irish Sea lies between Dublin and the English coast. It is only 60 miles wide. For more than 700 years, beginning in 1169, it served as an avenue for soldiers and settlers from England. The British made Ireland their colony. They seized Irish land and imposed harsh laws on the Irish people. The British ruled Ireland from their main stronghold, Dublin Castle. Dublin and the surrounding counties were known as "the obedient shires" because they were so firmly under British control.

The British settlers who made Ireland their home are referred to as the Anglo-Irish. Since 1534, most of the Anglo-Irish were Protestant, and the native Irish were Roman Catholic. The differences between the two groups often took the form of a religious conflict.

Time after time, the Irish rebelled against their British overlords. Time after time, they were defeated. After each rebellion, the British seized more land and passed more cruel laws. But every uprising produced new Irish heroes, heroes who inspired the next rebellion.

For Dubliners, the most revered hero of all is Theobald Wolfe Tone. Wolfe Tone, as he is usually called, was a handsome young lawyer. He dreamed of ending the strife between Catholics and Protestants in Ireland. In the early 1790s, he formed an organization called the United

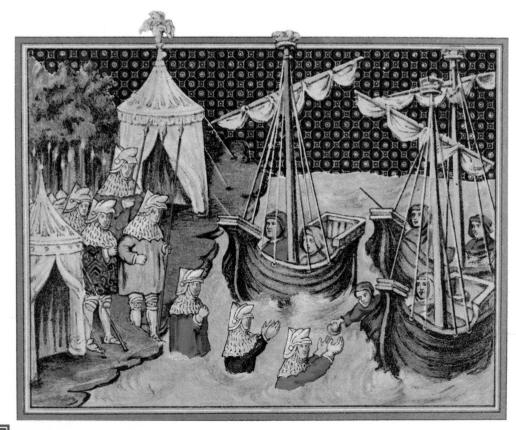

This 1394 color print shows ships bringing supplies to the English forces in Ireland.

Left: The English put down a series of Irish rebellions for more than 700 years, beginning in 1169. This woodcut shows the 1577 siege of Dublin.

Below: Theobald Wolfe Tone was captured by the English in 1798 after the rebellion of the United Irishmen failed.

Irishmen. Many Protestants feared the power of this new organization. With encouragement from the British throne, they made war on Wolfe Tone and his followers.

Hundreds of the United Irishmen were imprisoned in Dublin Castle. One jailer, known as Tom the Devil, invented a method of torture called the "pitch cap." A prisoner's hair was covered with pitch, sprinkled with gunpowder, and set ablaze. After looking in horror at a heap of bodies, one witness described the bloody scene as "the most frightful spectacle that ever disgraced a royal residence."

At last, Wolfe Tone himself was captured. Instead of giving him the honorable trial of a soldier, the British tried him as a common criminal. Wolfe Tone was condemned to be hanged as though he were a thief or a murderer. "I wish not for mercy," he said shortly before his death. "The favorite object of my life has been the independence of my country and to that object I have made every sacrifice."

THE EASTER RISING

On the morning of April 23, 1916, Dubliners put on their finest clothes and attended Easter Mass. Later, many set out for the racetrack to watch the Irish Grand National, the most important horse race of the year. As they hurried along Sackville Street (known as O'Connell Street today), a few people paused by the General Post Office. Standing before its columned facade, a man in a green uniform delivered a passionate speech. "Irish men and Irish women," the speaker cried, "in the name of God and of the dead generations from which she receives her old tradition of nationhood, Ireland, through us, summons her children to her flag and strikes for her freedom."

The people of Dublin were used to fiery speeches. For years, patriotic leaders had urged another rebellion. Few Dubliners suspected that the speech they heard that Easter morning was anything out of the ordinary. But those who listened closely heard something remarkable. The speaker, a thirty-six-year-old revolutionary named Patrick Pearse, announced that Ireland was now an independent republic. He declared that the ties with Great Britain were severed forever.

This special 1916 edition of Irish Life *told the story of what is now called the "Easter Rising."*

A view of the Dublin ruins after the Easter Rising

That afternoon, rebels attacked Dublin Castle, the hated symbol of British rule. The assault on the castle was unsuccessful. But the rebels managed to seize the General Post Office, the Imperial Hotel, and several other buildings. By the following day, Dublin was a city at war. Business came to a standstill. Fires flared in the streets, and looters rummaged through downtown stores. Shots ripped the air as British troops battled the Irish Volunteers and the Irish Citizens Army. Soon, the British outnumbered the rebels twenty to one. The rebels barricaded themselves in the General Post Office. The British bombarded the building with artillery fire. Within a week, Pearse and the other rebel leaders were captured. About 450 people, both Irish and British, were dead.

At first, most Dubliners resented the work of the rebels. But when Patrick Pearse and fourteen other rebel leaders were put to death, public feeling shifted. Like so many before them, the rebels became fallen heroes. Dubliners saw them as martyrs to the cause of Irish freedom.

The Easter Rising, as it was called, led to a full-scale war of independence. In 1921, all but six northern counties became the Irish Free State. The Irish Free State was a self-governing member of the British Commonwealth of Nations. British officials turned Dublin Castle over to the new Irish leaders.

Yet Dublin remained a city in turmoil. For two years, the Irish Free State was torn by civil war between Irish Catholics and Anglo-Irish Protestants. The fighting left many sections of Dublin in ruins.

At last, in 1937, the Republic of Ireland was born. The new constitution made no reference to Great Britain. Dublin was the capital of this new, independent nation. The six northern counties of Ireland, however remained under British rule.

Above: The Easter Rising of 1916 led to a major Irish war of independence. These Irish Republican Girl Raiders who held up a mail car in 1922 were looking for information about the English government.

The 1916 uprising has long been celebrated in drama and song. Dublin playwright Sean O'Casey called it "the Year One in Irish history and Irish life." But another Dublin writer, poet William Butler Yeats, remembered the tragedy as well as the glory. In his poem, *Easter 1916*, Yeats wrote:

I write it out in a verse —

MacDonagh and MacBride

And Connolly and Pearse

Now and in time to be,

Wherever green is worn,

Are changed, changed utterly:

A terrible beauty is born.

Top: Police trying to control a 1920 demonstration in Sackville Street

Left: A Dublin parade celebrating peace in December 1921

Early in the twentieth century, Irish patriots tried to revive the ancient Gaelic language. In general, the Gaelic Revival Movement was a failure. In Dublin, as in most of Ireland, English has come to stay. Nevertheless, a few Gaelic phrases still flavor Dublin speech. One such phrase is *ceol agus craic*, which means "music and fun." The city of Dublin offers ample portions of both.

ceol agus craic (KYOHL AH-GUSS KRAH-ICK)

THE LOVE OF A TALE

When Saint Patrick arrived to convert the Irish to Christianity, he decided to destroy their tales of pagan gods and heroes. His guardian angel stopped him just in time. The angel told Saint Patrick that these legends belonged to the Irish people, and must be preserved.

For centuries, wandering storytellers, or *shanachies*, kept the ancient tales alive. The storyteller might receive a few coins, or simply a meal and a warm place to spend the night. Over the years, the old tales were molded and reshaped like clay in a sculptor's hand.

At any Dublin festival today, there is bound to be a modern shanachie telling stories. People of all ages gather to hear of the *sidhe*, or fairies, who live in a secret world beneath our own. The audience listens to heroic legends of the magical hound named Cuchulain, and

shanachies (SHA-NAH-HEEZ)
sidhe (SHEE)
Cuchulain (KOO-HOO-LINN)
Tuatha (TOO-UH-HUH)
Lir (LEER)

Irish coins

People at the annual Dublin Street Fair

the vanished tribe called the Tuatha. Here and there, statues of these mythological figures grace Dublin's landscape. One of the most famous stands in Parnell Square. It depicts four figures that seem to be half swan and half human. The statue is based on the tale of the Children of Lir, four children who were changed into swans for 900 years. They regained their human form when they heard the pealing of bells from a Christian church.

With Dublin's love of storytelling, it is not surprising that the city has produced some of the finest writers of modern times. Many scholars consider James Joyce (1882-1941) to be the most important fiction writer of the twentieth century. Joyce's novels and short stories are filled with descriptions of Dublin streets, landmarks, and customs.

James Joyce, one of the most important fiction writers of the twentieth century, is shown here in a painting by Jeffrey Morgan and a statue on O'Connell Street.

Poets and playwrights also flourish in Dublin. The city has been home to four winners of the prestigious Nobel Prize for literature: playwrights George Bernard Shaw (1856-1950) and Samuel Beckett (1906-1989), and poets William Butler Yeats (1865-1939) and Seamus Heaney (1939-). Though Yeats is best remembered for his poems, he also wrote many plays and encouraged the rise of the theater in Dublin. In 1904, Yeats and a group of friends founded the Abbey Theatre, one of the most famous play-

A Jeffrey Morgan painting of playwright George Bernard Shaw

houses in the world. Born during the Gaelic Revival Movement, the theater put on plays in both Gaelic and English. Years later, Yeats remarked with pride, "I may say that we have turned a great deal of Irish imagination toward the stage."

Poet William Butler Yeats

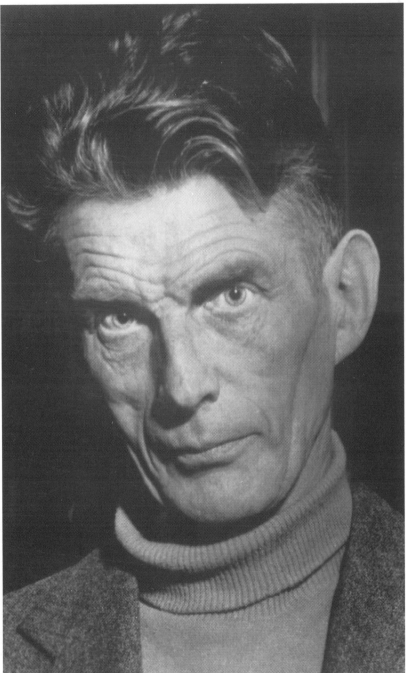

Playwright Samuel Beckett

PIPES AND DRUMS

Edward Martyn, a friend of Yeats, helped found the Abbey Theatre. Like Yeats, Martyn wanted to nourish Irish traditions in Dublin. To encourage traditional music and dance, he founded an annual celebration called the *Feis Ceol,* or Festival of Music. Today the Feis Ceol draws dancers and musicians from all over the world. The air rings with the sound of the *Uileann* pipes, which resemble Scottish bagpipes. Naturally, there are harpers; after all, the Irish harp is the oldest and most beloved instrument in the land. And, of course, there are fiddlers to make the music for jigs, reels, and other lively folk dances.

The Feis Ceol is only one of Dublin's many music festivals. But you don't have to go to a specially planned event to enjoy traditional songs. Dublin has dozens of "singing pubs." Anyone can join in on the choruses to old favorites, or simply sway and clap in rhythm.

Dublin also has a deep respect for classical music. In 1742, composer George Frideric Handel (1685-1759) conducted the world premiere of his masterpiece, the *Messiah,* at Dublin's Charitable Music Hall. With its breathtaking "Hallelujah Chorus," Handel's *Messiah* is one of the world's best-loved classical works.

Even children as young as this Irish girl grow up loving traditional Irish music of all kinds.

Feis Ceol (FESH KYOHL)
Uileann (ILL-INN)

Dubliners cherish tradition, but they also love anything that is new and exciting. Rock festivals lure vast crowds of young people to Dublin parks and concert halls. During the 1990s, the Dublin bands U2 and the Cranberries zoomed to worldwide fame. The dazzling popularity of these groups put Dublin at the center of the rock scene. Like rock musicians everywhere, Dubliners experiment with synthesized drum, guitar, and keyboard sounds. But at times, they turn back to the music of their ancestors. Here and there, the electronic blends of the nineties echo with the Irish harp and the Uileann pipes.

Young Dublin bagpipers

History Out of Tune

The Irish harp is a beautiful instrument that has been played for a thousand years. It is a symbol of Irish culture and the struggles of the country's people. The image of an Irish harp is carved on Dublin's monument to patriot Charles Parnell. But the sculptor was no musician. The strings of the carved harp are not attached properly to the instrument. If it were real, Parnell's harp would play very strange music.

GAMES AND RACES

Every August, talk in Dublin pubs turns to horses. Thousands of people pour into the city for the annual Dublin Horse Show. The show is held at the Royal Dublin Society on the eastern edge of the city. For six days, horses and riders compete in a series of races and dressage competitions. In dressage, riders are judged on the basis of proper form as they put their horses through complex turns and maneuvers. The crowning event of the show is the Nation's Cup, a grueling steeplechase. In this race, the horses must leap over a series of fourteen fences.

Jumping competition at the Dublin Horse Show

Riders and observers at the huge Dublin Horse Show, which is held over a period of six days every August and is attended by thousands of people

In addition to horse racing, Dubliners adore contact sports. The city sponsors five soccer teams, including the Dublin Shamrocks. Fans cheer wildly at soccer matches at the stadium at Dalymount Park. Rugby, a British import, is popular in South Dublin. Rugby was the ancestor of American football. It is a rough-and-tumble game in which the ball must be kicked, thrown, or carried past the opponent's goal. Some rugby formations look strange to spectators unused to the game. In one, the scrum, teammates form a tight line with their heads down. They look as though they are playing tug-of-war without a rope.

The Gaelic Athletic Association (GAA) was founded early in the twentieth century. As a matter of patriotism, the GAA spurred interest in traditional Irish sports. Its efforts met with spectacular success. Today, Dubliners play an assortment of uniquely Irish games. Among them are hurling, *camogie*, and Gaelic football.

Young rugby fans waving a team flag after a game

A rugby shirt

Anyone visiting Dublin should watch a hurling match.

Fans of Gaelic football say it is faster and more exciting than either soccer or rugby. In many ways, it is a cross between these two games, but it has fewer rules. Fifteen men play on a team. With lightning moves of their hands and feet, the players try to propel the ball through the goal, which looks like an upright letter H. Gaelic football isn't a game for sissies. When someone gets hurt, there are no time-outs. The game must go on, even while an injured player lies groaning on the field.

During the fourteenth century, English soldiers in Ireland were forbidden by law from playing in hurling matches. English officers claimed that passion for the game distracted the men from their military duties. To this day, hurling has an intensely passionate following. Enthusiasts insist it is the fastest game in the world. Hurling is somewhat like hockey. Players use a curved stick to strike a tiny, hard ball. The ball may also be thrown or kicked to a goal.

Camogie is a form of hurling played by women. It is much like the men's game, but uses a lighter stick. No visitor to Dublin will want to leave without watching a hurling match. But hurling is only one of the many attractions of this fascinating city.

In Dublin, June 16 is known as Bloomsday. Book lovers gather for a pilgrimage through the city's streets. They follow the wanderings of Leopold Bloom, the main character in *Ulysses*, James Joyce's classic novel. The book takes place in Dublin on June 16, 1904. Joyce once remarked that if Dublin were destroyed, it could be rebuilt brick by brick by following the descriptions in *Ulysses*.

Dublin has changed since Joyce's day. But it still offers a wealth of wonderful things to see and do.

CENTRAL DUBLIN

On a clear day in Dublin, the River Liffey is alive with rowboats and sailing craft. Here and there, people fish from the quays along its banks. The Custom House, one of Dublin's landmark buildings, looms at the river's mouth. To most Dubliners, the Liffey is the dividing line that cuts their city into two distinct sections, north and south. The oldest part of the city, hugging the river on both sides, is known as Central Dublin. Central Dublin is so compact that it can be crossed in a fifteen-minute walk. Yet it is one of the most interesting areas of the city.

The River Liffey

Right: This arch is the gateway to St. Stephen's Green.

Below: This girl was in a wedding party held at St. Stephen's Green.

At Dublin's heart lies St. Stephen's Green, a 27-acre park laid out in 1664. At the park's entrance stands the Fusiliers' Arch, a memorial to Irish troops who fought with the British during the Boer War in South Africa. Because of anti-British feeling in Dublin, it is somerimes called the Traitors' Arch. St. Stephen's Green is a lovely park full of ponds and gardens. Here and there, statues honor some of Dublin's greats and near-greats: James Joyce, William Butler Yeats, Theobald Wolfe Tone. One statue represents Constance Gore Booth, also known as Countess Markiewicz. Countess Markiewicz was an Irish woman who married a Polish aristocrat. She marched with the rebels in the 1916 Rising.

St. Stephen's Green is surrounded by elegant old houses, many dating back to the eighteenth century. Ely House, built in 1771, serves as headquarters for a Catholic organization called the Knights of Columbus. In the entrance hall is a magnificent statue of the Greek hero Hercules. Panels depicting Hercules's superhuman adventures line the walls up the stairs. The banisters are carved in the form of writhing serpents.

A statue of patriot Robert Emmet stands in St. Stephen's Green, near the house where he once lived. Its inscription comes from the last speech Emmet gave before he was beheaded by the British: "When my country takes her place among the nations of the earth, then and not till then let my epitaph be written."

The National Museum of Ireland is one of the finest museums in Europe. On display are many archaeological finds from Irish sites, including priceless gold ornaments 3,000 years old. Among the museum's treasures is the Ardagh Chalice, a jeweled cup that was discovered in 1867 by a boy digging potatoes. Traditional crafts such as lace and glassware are also on exhibit. One room is dedicated to pictures and memorabilia from the Easter Rising of 1916.

Grafton Street, one of Dublin's main thoroughfares, is both lively and stylish. It is lined with boutiques, bookstores, and antique shops. Jugglers and musicians perform on the sidewalks. Every now and then, someone ventures to recite an original poem to the passersby. On one corner stands a statue of Molly Malone, who once sold cockles and mussels on the streets of "Dublin's fair city."

Ardagh (ARR-DUH)

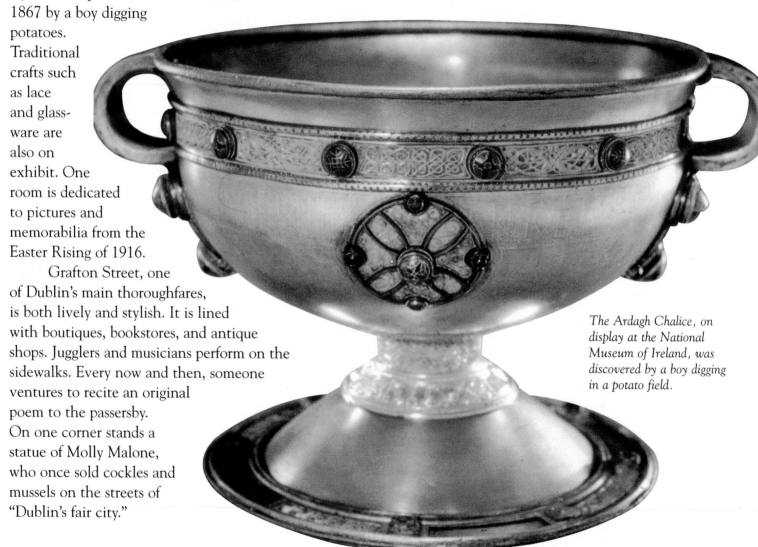

The Ardagh Chalice, on display at the National Museum of Ireland, was discovered by a boy digging in a potato field.

A young Dublin musician

This handkerchief is made of Irish linen and is trimmed with a traditional Irish lace pattern.

SOUTH DUBLIN

The original portion of Christ Church Cathedral was built in the year 1172, making it the oldest church in Dublin. Christ Church overflows with plaques, paintings, and statues. One of the most beloved is the carved figure of a weeping child, with a teardrop sliding down its cheek. In one of the cathedral's many chapels hangs a bronze case containing the

Christ Church Cathedral, shown here, is the oldest church in Dublin.

St. Patrick's Cathedral

embalmed heart of Saint Lawrence O'Toole, the patron saint of Dublin. A crypt beneath the floor holds an extraordinary collection of relics, including the skeleton of a cat that was once found among the pipes of the cathedral's organ.

Jonathan Swift is best known as the author of *Gulliver's Travels*, the tale of a sailor's adventures among people six inches tall. Swift is buried in St. Patrick's Cathedral, where he served as dean from 1713 to 1745. A church has stood on this spot since the fifth century A.D., when Saint Patrick converted the Irish to Christianity. St. Patrick's is crowned by a magnificent spire that is 105 feet tall.

Construction on Dublin Castle began in 1204 by orders of England's King John, "as well to curb the city as to defend it." For centuries, the castle was the hated symbol of British oppression. After each new uprising, the heads of rebels were impaled on spikes along its outer walls. Today, the castle is mainly used for public ceremonies.

During the eighteenth century, Merrion Square became the fashionable center of Anglo-Irish life. The square is surrounded by houses from this period, known as the Georgian Era after King

Dublin Castle

George III of England. Georgian houses are three or four stories high with wide granite steps and porches. Most of them have a window with decorative plasterwork above the front door. On summer weekends, artists flock to Merrion Square to display their work. Paintings for sale hang from the railings around the park.

Among Dublin's most charming neighborhoods is Temple Bar. In the 1960s, authorities wanted to level this area to make room for a new bus terminal. Protesters saved Temple Bar from being demolished. With its narrow cobblestone streets and original storefronts, Temple Bar looks much as it did in the eighteenth century. Musicians cluster at the Merchant's Arch, playing fiddles, pipes, or electric guitars. Galleries display the work of local artists and craftspeople.

Above left: A typical Merrion Square Georgian doorway

Right: A Merrion Square door knocker

Left: Flowers in a Merrion Square park

Children in Phoenix Park

Dublin's history is full of sorrow. It is not surprising that one of the city's major landmarks is a graveyard. Glasnevin Cemetery is the final resting place of many of Dublin's heroes. Every Dublin schoolchild knows their names: Charles Parnell, Eamon de Valera, Daniel O'Connell. O'Connell's tomb dominates the grounds. It is a huge round tower 16 stories high.

From the top of a pillar in Phoenix Park, a bronze bird rises from bronze flames. The statue depicts the phoenix, a legendary bird that is reborn from its own ashes. But Phoenix Park is not named for

Glasnevin (GLAHSS-NEH-VINN)
fionn uisce (FINN ISH-KIH)

this mythical bird at all. The name actually comes from the Gaelic words *fionn uisce,* meaning "clear water." Phoenix Park sprawls over 1,752 acres along the south bank of the River Liffey. During the Middle Ages, it was the private domain of an order of knights called the Knights Hospitalers. Anyone caught poaching deer in the park would be hanged. Today, there are still deer, but Phoenix Park belongs to all the people of Dublin. It is the backyard and playground for the whole city.

Phoenix Park is a medley of woods and meadows where visitors can forget the stress of city life. Within the park is the 30-acre Dublin Zoo. The zoo specializes in breeding endangered species. In 1931, it was the birthplace of the MGM lion, whose roar opens hundreds of classic films. The Heritage Trail highlights the park's

many historic monuments. Chief among them is the Wellington Testimonial, a granite obelisk soaring 205 feet into the sky. The obelisk commemorates Lord Wellington, the British general who defeated Emperor Napoleon Bonaparte in 1812.

The Wellington Testimonial (right) is one of the monuments in Phoenix Park (below).

"Bananas, bananas! . . . Chocolate, delicious chocolate!" On Moore and Henry Streets, the air rings with the cries of vendors. This patch of North Dublin is an outdoor market, completely closed to car traffic. Vendors specialize in tobacco, fruit, cheese, chocolate, and many other goods. Visitors are warned to beware of "dippers," or pickpockets, who slip through the crowds.

A few blocks east of the market, O'Connell Street cuts its way through North Dublin. Visitors often pause to gaze at the General Post Office, where Patrick Pearse declared Irish independence in 1916. Along the center island, statues and monuments honor Dublin's rebel heroes. At the Anna Livia Fountain, young men and women gather to decide where they will go from here.

The Moore Street outdoor fruit and vegetable market in North Dublin is completely closed to traffic.

The Banishment of Tumult

When Trinity College opened in Dublin in 1592, its founders had high ideals. They meant the college to be a place "whereby knowledge, learning, and civility may be increased, to the banishment of barbarism, tumult, and disorderly living." For 400 years, Trinity College has been Dublin's most respected university. But the students have not always been orderly. In the eighteenth century, a notice in the dining hall stated that "no student shall walk over the dinner tables and there shall be no throwing of bread."

The General Post Office on O'Connell Street, where Patrick Pearse declared Irish independence

FAMOUS LANDMARKS

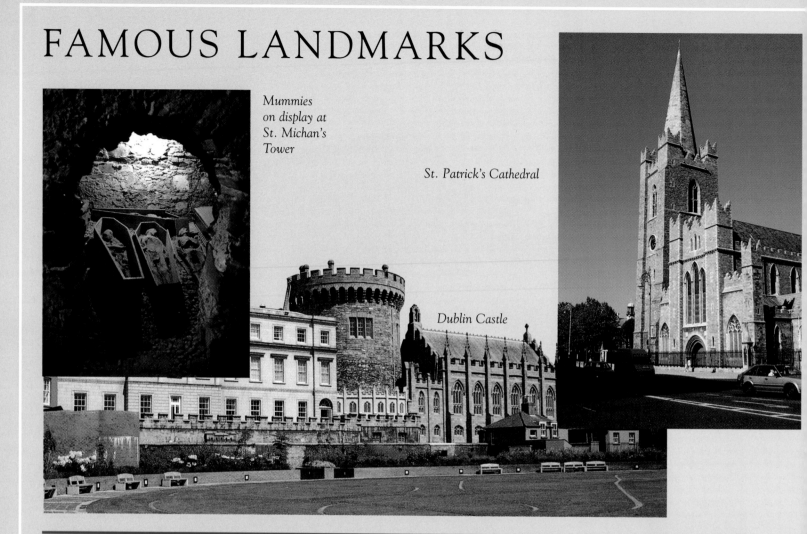

Mummies on display at St. Michan's Tower

St. Patrick's Cathedral

Dublin Castle

Phoenix Park
The largest city park in Europe, covering 1,752 acres. The park contains many historic monuments and the home of Ireland's president. Anglo-Irish aristocrats fought duels here during the eighteenth century.

Dublin Castle
Once the hated center of British authority in Ireland. The castle was completed in 1268. Today, it is used mainly for ceremonial occasions and international conferences.

National Gallery
Ireland's leading museum of art. It features painting and sculpture by Irish artists, as well as works by Impressionists and Renaissance masters. The museum is partially supported by the estate of playwright George Bernard Shaw. Shaw's statue stands outside the entrance.

Garden of Remembrance
Garden in Parnell Square. It was established to honor those who died in the 1916 Rising.

Christ Church Cathedral
Dublin's oldest surviving church. Work on the cathedral began in 1172. One chapel contains the embalmed heart of Saint Lawrence O'Toole, Dublin's patron saint.

Kilmainham Prison Museum
Formerly Kilmainham Gaol. The leaders of the 1916 Rising were executed here in the Killing Courtyard. The museum traces the grim history of the prison from 1792 to 1922.

Royal Kilmainham Hospital
Now serves as a museum of modern art. Heroes of the 1916 Rising are buried on the grounds. The building originally served as a home for wounded veterans.

St. Patrick's Cathedral
The largest church in Ireland. The cathedral stands near the place where Saint Patrick is said to have preached. Within the church is the tomb of Jonathan Swift, who served as dean from 1713 to 1745.

*Interior of the
National Gallery*

The Four Courts Building

Glasnevin Cemetery
Dublin's most historic graveyard. It is the final resting place of many Irish patriots, including Eamon de Valera, Charles Parnell, and Daniel O'Connell.

General Post Office
Scene of the historic proclamation of Irish independence on Easter Sunday, 1916. The columned facade is a landmark on O'Connell Street.

National Museum of Ireland
Museum of art and history. The collections include many Irish archaeological treasures, some dating back 3,000 years. One room is dedicated to memorabilia of the 1916 Rising.

Custom House
Massive arcaded building dating to 1791. The building is decorated by the work of Dublin sculptor Edward Smith. Today, it houses Ireland's Department of the Environment.

St. Michan's Tower
Contains vaults full of mummified corpses. Bodies buried nearby were mummified due to the mineral content of the soil. Many of the mummies are on display.

Four Courts Building
Imposing 1744 building containing Ireland's Supreme Court. Much of the original structure was burned during the 1922-1924 civil war. Thousands of priceless historical records were lost forever.

Irish National War Memorial Gardens
Commemorates the Irish soldiers who died during World War I. Two pavilions contain massive volumes with the names of more than 150,000 people who lost their lives.

Dublin Civic Museum
Museum tracing the history of Dublin. It displays pictures, newspaper stories, and other relics of Dublin's past.

FAST FACTS

POPULATION   **1995**

City: 502,749
Metropolitan Area: 866,241

AREA   45 square miles

LOCATION Dublin is the capital of the Republic of Ireland, or Eire. It lies on Dublin Bay at the mouth of the River Liffey on Ireland's eastern coast. The Wicklow Mountains fringe the city to the south and west.

CLIMATE Dublin has a mild, moist climate. Light rain is frequent throughout the year. January temperatures average 40 degrees Fahrenheit. In July, the average temperature is 60 degrees Fahrenheit.

ECONOMY About one-fourth of Ireland's manufacturing is based in Dublin. Factories produce chemicals, clothing, electrical and electronic equipment, furniture, machinery, metal products, printed material, processed foods, textiles, and tobacco. As a seaport, Dublin handles half of Ireland's foreign trade.

CHRONOLOGY

200 B.C.
Celtic people from France and Spain arrive in Ireland

A.D. 432
Saint Patrick brings Christianity to Ireland; he preaches near the site of today's St. Patrick's Cathedral

A.D. 837
Viking invaders found Dublin at the mouth of the Liffey

1014
Brian Boru, high king of Ireland, defeats the Vikings at Clontarf, north of Dublin

1171
Dublin falls to invaders from Britain

1172
Construction begins on Christ Church Cathedral

1190
St. Patrick's Cathedral is founded

1268
Dublin Castle, the stronghold of English rule, is completed

1592
Trinity College is founded

1649-1652
After the English Civil War, Oliver Cromwell unleashes a reign of terror in Ireland; some 600,000 people die as a result

1742
Handel's *Messiah* premieres at Dublin's Charitable Music Hall

1803
Irish nationalists led by Robert Emmet attempt a coup in Dublin; Emmet is executed

1823
Daniel O'Connell leads a campaign for Catholic rights

The Custom House, on the River Liffey, was designed by English architect James Grandon.

1845-49
One million people die in a famine when a fungus destroys Ireland's potato crop; another million leave the country

1881
Charles Stuart Parnell is imprisoned in Dublin's Kilmainham Jail for encouraging unrest

1904
William Butler Yeats and others establish the Abbey Theatre

1916
Rebels seize 14 buildings in Dublin during the Easter Rising; 15 rebel leaders are executed

1919
The Irish Free State is formed as part of the British Commonwealth; Eamon de Valera is elected president

1921
Twenty-six counties in southern Ireland form the Republic of Ireland; 6 counties in the north remain tied to Great Britain

1922-1924
Ireland is torn by civil war; much of Dublin is destroyed

1937
A new Irish constitution is ratified; it severs the last ties between Great Britain and the Republic of Ireland

1966
A bomb blast destroys Nelson's Column on O'Connell Street, to Irish nationalists a symbol of British oppression

1979
1.2 million people gather in Phoenix Park to welcome Pope John Paul II

1991
Artists and writers raise funds to open the National Poetry Center in Temple Bar

DUBLIN

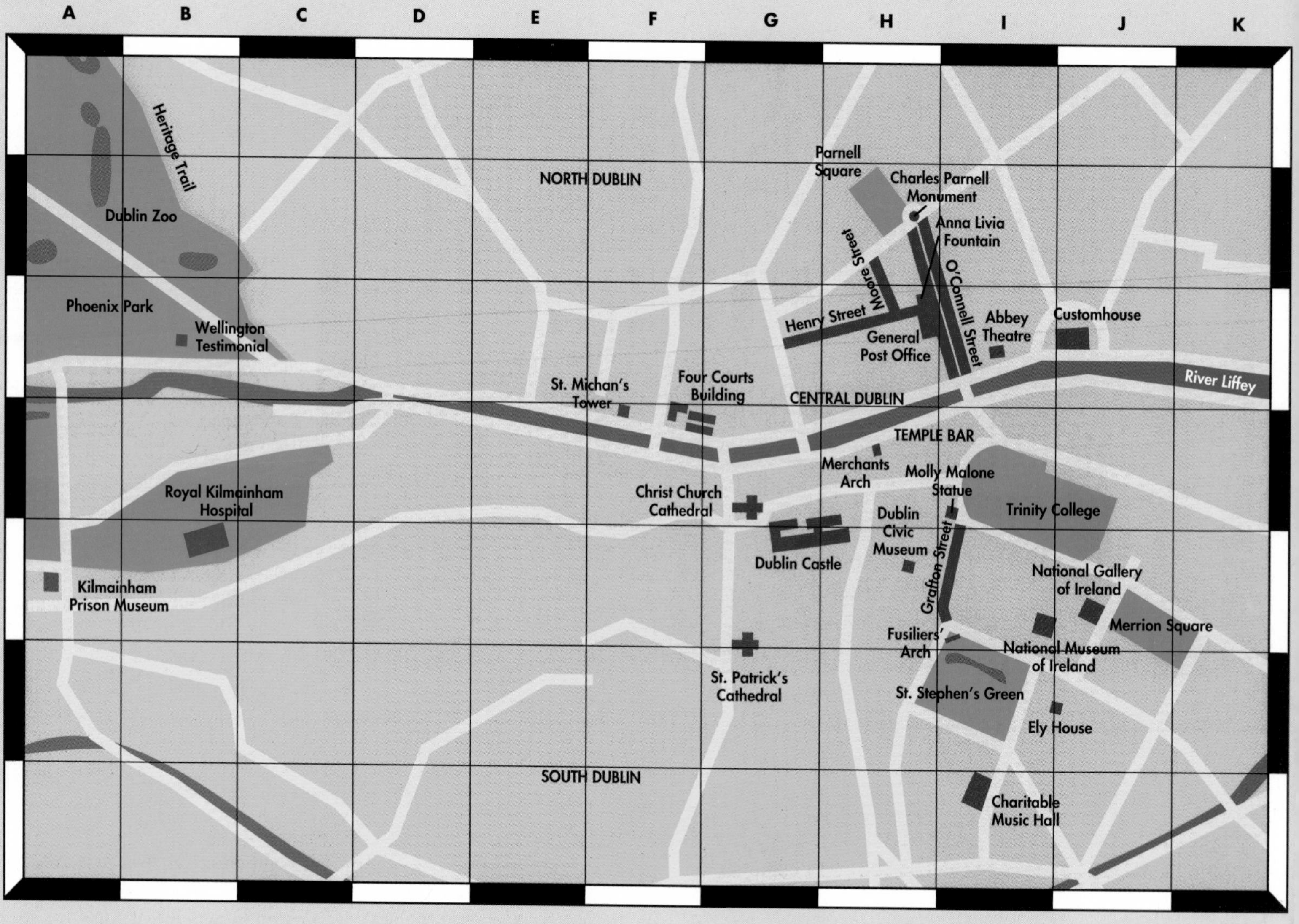
A
B
C
D
E
F
G
H
I
J
K
1
2
3
4
5
6
7
Heritage Trail
Dublin Zoo
Phoenix Park
Wellington Testimonial
NORTH DUBLIN
Parnell Square
Charles Parnell Monument
Anna Livia Fountain
Moore Street
O'Connell Street
Henry Street
General Post Office
Abbey Theatre
Customhouse
River Liffey
St. Michan's Tower
Four Courts Building
CENTRAL DUBLIN
TEMPLE BAR
Merchants Arch
Molly Malone Statue
Royal Kilmainham Hospital
Christ Church Cathedral
Trinity College
Dublin Civic Museum
Grafton Street
Dublin Castle
National Gallery of Ireland
Kilmainham Prison Museum
Merrion Square
Fusiliers' Arch
National Museum of Ireland
St. Patrick's Cathedral
St. Stephen's Green
Ely House
SOUTH DUBLIN
Charitable Music Hall

Abbey Theatre	I3	Dublin Castle	G,H 4,5	Grafton Street	I5
Anna Livia Fountain	H3	Dublin Civic Museum	H5	Henry Street	G,H 3
Central Dublin	G,H 3	Dublin Zoo	A,B 2	Heritage Trail	A,B,C 1,2,3
Charitable Music Hall	I7	Ely House	I,J6	Irish Sea	O1
Charles Parnell Monument	H2	Four Courts Building	F,G 4	Kilmainham Prison Museum	A5
Christ Church Cathedral	G6	Fusiliers' Arch	I5	Merchants Arch	H4
Custom House	J3	General Post Office	H3	Merrion Square	J,K 4,5
Dublin Bay	M,N,O 2,3,4	Glasnevin Cemetery	L2	Molly Malone Statue	I4

DUBLIN AND SURROUNDINGS

GLOSSARY

baritone: Male vocal range, higher than a bass

contemplation: Deep thought

eccentric: Person who habitually behaves in a peculiar manner

epitaph: Words written on a tombstone

facade: Decorative front of a building

haven: Safe retreat

inscription: Carved words on a monument

martyr: Person who dies for a cause

minute: Tiny

monastery: Place where monks live apart from the world

obelisk: Tall, tapered 4-sided stone pillar with a pyramid-shaped cap

oppressor: Person who cruelly dominates another

saber: Long curved sword

tolerant: Accepting

tumult: Noise and confusion

vibrant: Brimming with life and excitement

Picture Identifications

Cover: Trinity College, George Bernard Shaw statue at the National Gallery, two Irish children
Page 3: Girl Guides on an outing
Pages 4-5: O'Connell Street
Pages 8-9: Schoolgirls on a Dublin tour
Pages 18-19: Performing an Irish jig for royal visitors, 1871
Pages 30-31: A Dublin flower vendor
Pages 42-43: The River Liffey and Four Courts

INDEX

Page numbers in boldface type indicate illustrations

TO FIND OUT MORE

BOOKS

A Day in the Life of Ireland. San Francisco: Collins Publishers, 1991.

Bunn, Mike. *Ireland: The Taste and the Country.* London: Anaya Publishers Limited, 1991.

Christmas in Ireland. Chicago: World Book, Inc., 1985.

Cullen, Paul and Ken Boyle. *Direct from Ireland: Dublin.* Lincolnwood, Ill.: Passport Books, 1995.

Dunlop, Eileen. *Tales of St. Patrick.* New York: Holiday House, 1995.

Fradin, Dennis. *Ireland.* Enchantment of the World series. Chicago: Childrens Press, 1984.

Gerard-Sharp, Lisa and Tim Perry. *Ireland.* Eye Witness Travel Guides. New York: Dorling Kindersley, 1995.

Grenham, John. *Tracing Your Irish Ancestors.* Baltimore: Genealogical Publishing Co., Inc., 1992.

Nardo, Don. *The Irish Potato Famine.* San Diego: Lucent Books, 1990.

Neville, Peter. *A Traveller's History of Ireland.* New York: Interlink Books, 1995.

O'Brien, Jacqueline with Desmond Guinness. *Dublin: A Grand Tour.* New York: Harry N. Abrams, 1994.

Peplow, Mary and Debra Shipley. *Ireland.* World in View series. Austin, Texas: Steck Vaughn, 1989.

ONLINE SITES

Cathedrals and Churches
http://www.hoi.ie/dubguide/churches.htm
History and description of the most notable houses of worship in Dublin

City.net: Dublin
http://www.city.net/countries/ireland/dublin/
City information, yellow and white pages, arts and entertainment, weather, sightseeing, maps — and even your horoscope!

Dublin
http://ireland.iol.ie/~discover/dubsee.htm
Visit the 200-year-old Custom House, the National Library, and dozens of other Dublin landmarks

Dublin Chamber of Commerce
http://www.dubchamber.ie/
Mostly business-related, but some good stuff on travel and events in Dublin; read *Chamber Magazine*

Dublin City University
http://www.dcu.ie/
Find out what's going on at DCU: general information, messages from the president, people searches, and more

Guide to Dublin
http://www.hoi.ie/dubguide/dubindex.htm
Museums, churches, cultural sites, public buildings, Old Dublin, and more

Irish Music on the Web
http://www.bess.tcd.ie/music.htm
Enjoy everything from Celtic music to modern favorites, along with the Irish National Anthem in Irish and English

The Irish Times
http://www.irish-times.com/
Find out what's happening all over Ireland with this online newspaper

Irish Universities
http://www.bess.tcd.ie/univ.htm
Link up with the major colleges and universities in Ireland, or go on a virtual tour of the country

ABOUT THE AUTHOR

Deborah Kent grew up in Little Falls, New Jersey, and received a B.A. in English from Oberlin College. She earned a master's degree from Smith College School for Social Work. After working for four years at the University Settlement House in New York City, she moved to San Miguel de Allende in central Mexico. There she wrote her first young-adult novel, *Belonging*.

Ms. Kent is the author of more than a dozen young-adult novels, as well as numerous nonfiction titles for children. She lives in Chicago with her husband, children's book author R. Conrad Stein, and their daughter Jana.

AAu 2637